To:

From

*Our lives are filled with simple joys
and blessings without end,
And one of the greatest joys in life
is to have a friend.*

Some people are so special that once they enter your life, it becomes richer and fuller and more wonderful than you ever thought it could be.

The way from God to a person's heart
is through another person's heart.

*I thank God,
my friend,
for the blessing
you are...
for the joy of your
laughter...
the comfort of
your prayers...
and the warmth of
your smile.*

The friend who is really worth having is the one who will listen to your deepest hurts and feel they are hers too.

A friend is someone who comes in when the whole world has gone out.

Those who bring sunshine to the lives of others cannot keep it from themselves.

James M. Barrie

*I've never said all
the things I wish
I would have, but
I thank you for all
the times you
understood.*

Friendship brings people close no matter how great the distance between them.

*When hands reach out in friendship,
hearts are touched with joy.*

The more I know you, the more
I want to know you more.

Roy Lessin

To have a friend is to have one of the sweetest gifts that life can bring.

Amy Robertson Brown

Your own sky will lighten, if other skies
you brighten by just being happy
with a heart full of song.

Ripley D. Saunders

*A friend understands what you
are trying to say...even when your
thoughts aren't fitting into words.*

Ann D. Parrish

*Friendship doubles our joys
and divides our griefs.*

A friend is a person with a sneaky knack of saying good things about you behind your back.

*You're special—not because I've said so,
but because forever and always you've
been a part of God's plan.*

*A friend is one who knows
all about you and won't go away.*

*Blessed are they who have the gift
of making friends, for it is one
of God's best gifts.*

Thomas Hughes

Friendship is a gift from God that's blessed in every part... born through love and loyalty... conceived within the heart.

*There is nothing better than the
encouragement of a good friend.*

Katherine Butler Hathaway

*Good times with you are
the best times in life.*

Friends...they cherish each other's hopes.
They are kind to each other's dreams.

Henry David Thoreau

A good friend remembers what we were and sees what we can be.

Janette Oke

*There is no friend like the old friend who
has shared our morning days.*

Oliver Wendell Holmes

*A friend is one who believes in you
before you believe in yourself.*

*Until we meet again, may God hold
you in the palm of His hand.*

They are rich who have friends.

Scandinavian Proverb

*Two are better than one...for if they fall,
one will lift up the other.*

Ecclesiastes 4:9,10 *NRSV*

*Moments shared with you are
refreshing streams of Heaven's Light.*

*Friends warm you with their presence,
trust you with their secrets, and
remember you in their prayers.*

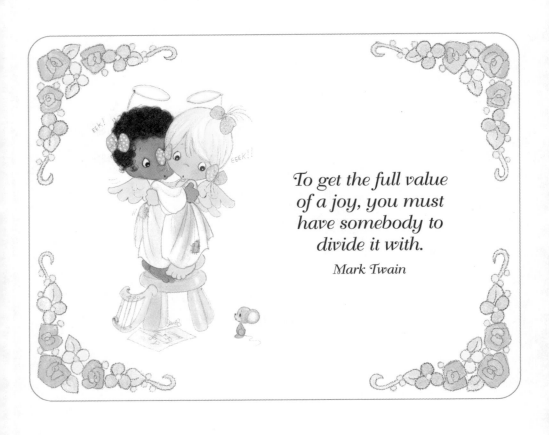

To get the full value of a joy, you must have somebody to divide it with.

Mark Twain

*Of all happinesses, the most charming is
that of a firm and gentle friendship.*

Seneca

I think of you often. Whether we're near or far apart, we always keep each other in our hearts.

Friends will not only live in harmony, but in melody.

Henry David Thoreau

*Your friendship
helps me get over
the rough spots
in life.*

Friendship is won not by the giving of things, but by the giving of the heart.

Roy Lessin

A friend loveth at all times.

Proverbs 17:17 KJV

A loyal friend is like a safe shelter;
find one, and you have found a treasure.

Sirach

*True friends are
never far apart,
each keeps the other
in her heart.*

*Friends believe in your dreams
as much as you do.*

*My friend shall forever be my friend
and reflect a ray of God to me.*

Henry David Thoreau

*Life's pleasures are multiplied when
we stick together with our friends.*

Friendship is sharing openly, laughing often, trusting always, caring deeply.

Instead of a gem or even a flower,
cast the gift of a lovely thought
into the heart of a friend.

George MacDonald

*Friendship is having a
shoulder to lean on.*

*Friendship is precious, not only in the
shade, but in the sunshine of life.*

Thomas Jefferson

Be kind and
compassionate
to one another.

Ephesians 4:32 NIV

*One of life's greatest treasures is the love
that binds hearts together in friendship.*

*As fire and hearth are inseparable,
so are the hearts of faithful friends.*

Blessed are the ones God sends to show His love for us...our friends.

A friend is one to whom one may pour out all the contents of one's heart...knowing that gentle hands will take and sift it, [and] keep what is worth keeping.

George Eliot

*A friend is one who listens
with her heart.*

A friend is dearer than the light of heaven; for it would be better for us that the sun were extinguished, than that we should be without friends.

Chrysostom

Of all the best things upon the earth,
I hold that a faithful friend is the best.

Edward Bulwer-Lytton

*Thoughtfulness
is to friendship
what sunshine is
to a garden.*

The best mirror is an old friend.

English Proverb

*May the Lord watch between you
and me when we are absent
one from another.*

Genesis 31:49 NKJV

*A cup of tea, a prayer or two,
blessed moments shared with you.*

Ellen Cuomo

Knowing what to say is not always necessary; just the presence of a caring friend can make a world of difference.

Sheri Curry

*You put a song in my heart
and sunshine in my sky.*

*Let not the grass grow on
the path of friendship.*

Native American Proverb

*Friendship is a hug
just when it is needed.*

They say you will never be lonely from the start of each day to its end if you walk life's pathway with love in your heart, and side by side with a friend.

Together we stick; divided we're stuck.

Evon Hedly

Bear ye one another's burdens.

Galatians 6:2 KJV

*All we have and are is a gift
of grace to be shared.*

Lloyd John Ogilvie

Everyone was meant to share God's all-abiding love and care; He saw that we would need to know a way to let these feelings show... So God made hugs.

Jill Wolf

After the friendship of God, a friend's affection is the greatest treasure we have.

Those who sow courtesy reap friendship,
and those who plant kindness gather love.

My best praise is that I am your friend.

Southerne

Friendship is a cozy shelter from life's rainy days.

Dear friends are never forgotten:
they live within your heart.

Pleasant words are a honeycomb,
sweet to the soul and healing.

Proverbs 16:24 NIV

*One friend ever watches and
cares for another.*

Randle Cosgrave

*I remember the times
you were there for me,
showing real interest
and concern.*

I'm thankful for the closeness we share.
How I enjoy being with you!

There is no joy in life like the joy of sharing.

Billy Graham

*A friend is a gift whose worth
is measured by the heart.*

A friend is a close companion on rainy days, someone to share with through every phase... Forgiving and helping to bring out the best, believing the good and forgetting the rest.

*Encourage each other to build
each other up.*

1 Thessalonians 5:11 *NIV*

*Friendship is the golden thread that
ties the hearts of all the world.*

John Evelyn

*A friend is what the heart
needs all the time.*

Henry van Dyke

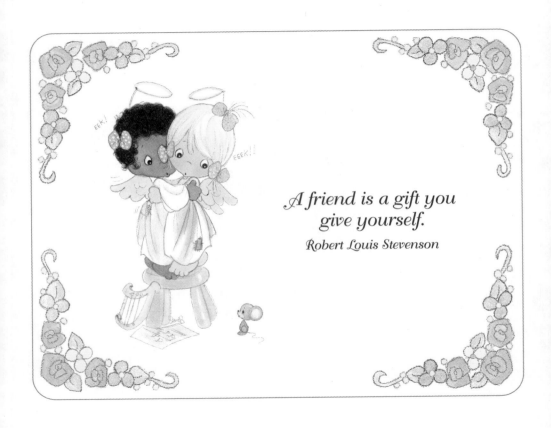

A friend is a gift you give yourself.

Robert Louis Stevenson

*If I had a single flower for
every time I think about you,
I could walk forever in my garden.*

Claudia A. Grandi

*I appreciate your thoughtfulness
and kind ways. I appreciate all the
things you do and all the ways
you show that you care.*

Roy Lessin

*We have been friends together
in sunshine and in shade.*

Caroline Norton

Every moment is full of wonder, and God is always present.

*When just being together is more
important than what you do,
you are with a friend.*

*Be full of sympathy toward each other,
loving one another with tender
hearts and humble minds.*

1 Peter 3:8 *TLB*

*You're my friend—what a thing
friendship is, world without end!*

Robert Browning

Favorite people,
favorite places,
favorite memories
of the past...
these are the joys
of a lifetime...
these are the things
that last.

May life's greatest gifts always be yours—
happiness, memories, and dreams.

*When you hold a hand that needs you,
you'll discover abundant joy.*